FAMOUS PEOPLE
FAMOUS LIVES

KU-626-820

Biographies of famous people to
support the curriculum.

James
Watt

by Nicola Baxter
Illustrations by Martin Remphry

W
FRANKLIN WATTS
LONDON•SYDNEY

First published in 2000
by Franklin Watts
This edition 2002

Franklin Watts
96 Leonard Street
London EC2A 4XD

Franklin Watts Australia
56 O'Riordan Street
Alexandria, Sydney
NSW 2015

ISBN 0 7496 4344 7 (pbk)

A CIP catalogue record for this book is
available from the British Library

Dewey Decimal Classification
Number: 621.21

Editor: Louise John

Printed in Great Britain

James Watt

On 19th January 1736, Agnes Watt sighed as she held her new baby son. "We'll call him James," she said, "like his father. And we'll take great care of him."

Her husband knew she was thinking of their other babies that had not survived.

James grew up in the fishing port of Greenock, on the coast of Scotland. His father started out as a carpenter, but was soon making and supplying all sorts of goods to fishermen and builders.

Agnes looked after her son very carefully, but he was often ill. As he grew up, he suffered badly from toothache and headaches.

You're too delicate to send to school. We'll teach you at home.

When he was healthy, young James learned quickly. As well as the lessons his mother taught him, he loved to make things in his father's workshop.

Later, James did go to school,
but he seemed slow and
awkward … except in maths
lessons. There he was brilliant!

As he grew older, James still enjoyed working in his father's workshop. He loved to repair the scientific instruments that sailors used, such as compasses and telescopes.

Then, when James was seventeen, his life changed. His mother died and his father lost most of his money. After a while, James decided to go to London to learn to make scientific instruments.

James bought himself a horse and set off. The journey took him twelve long days.

9

In London things were not easy for James. The only instrument-maker who agreed to train him said that he must work without pay for a whole year.

James was desperate, so he agreed. He soon impressed his employer, John Morgan, with his hard work and skill.

James worked hard. He wanted to squeeze the usual seven years of training into one year. He had little money for food. At the end of the year, he was very ill.

Now aged twenty, James returned home. Back in Scotland, he soon felt much better. He went to the thriving city of Glasgow to find work in his new trade.

At this time, Glasgow's busy port was trading with the West Indies and the growing colonies of America. James was lucky to be given a job at the university, repairing some scientific instruments that had been sent over from Jamaica.

These instruments have been damaged by salt water. See if you can put them right.

James did the job so well that he was made 'Mathematical Instrument Maker to the University'. Now he was able to meet and talk with famous scientists there. He learnt a lot from them and they admired his knowledge and skill.

Things were going well for James in other ways, too. He moved to a new workshop where he eventually employed sixteen men.

And in 1765, he married his cousin, Margaret Miller.

One day in 1763, Professor John Anderson, an old friend, brought James a working model to repair. It was of an early type of steam engine called a Newcomen engine.

They failed to mend this in London. See what you can do, James.

The full-sized Newcomen engine was used to pump water out of Cornish mines. James Watt was fascinated by what he saw.

When water is boiled, it turns into a gas called steam. Steam takes up much, much more space than water – about 1,700 times as much. If the steam is trapped in a container and then quickly cooled, it turns back into water.

The Newcomen engine used this method to pump water, but it did not work very well. It also needed a huge amount of coal to keep it moving. James set out to find a way of improving it.

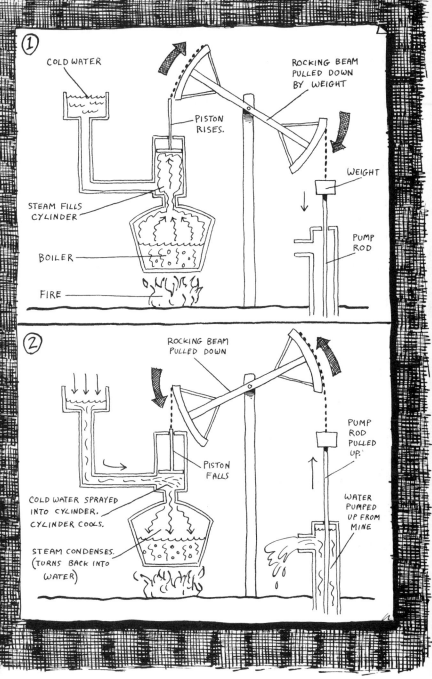

How the Newcomen engine works

James thought about the problem for months. The answer came one Sunday afternoon in May 1765. James was taking a walk across Glasgow Green when he had a brilliant idea.

Even so, it was many years before he managed to make his idea work properly. These were difficult years for James, who now had two small children to support. To make ends meet, he took on surveying work for the people building new canals.

If only I could get back to work on the steam engine.

James was thirty-five now and he was often depressed by his work. Everything seemed to take so long. His wife did her best to keep him cheerful.

Then, in 1774, James's wife died. There was nothing to keep him in Scotland now. He knew there was a man in Birmingham, who wanted to help him with money and ideas. James packed up and moved south with his children.

The man in Birmingham was called Matthew Boulton. He was a wealthy factory-owner with a great interest in science. He also liked finding new ways to make money! This was just the kind of partner James needed.

We can do great things together, James. Your work is so important.

At last! Someone who understands.

Matthew Boulton's factory at Soho, just outside Birmingham, was very modern for its time. Boulton at once showed his faith in James's new engine by setting it up to pump water for his own factory. It was a great success.

Soon it was time for the Boulton & Watt pumping engine to be tested in public. An excited crowd gathered at the Bloomfield coal mine. Would the engine work?

In the engine house, the heat from the boiler was terrible. The engineer checked a gauge and pulled a lever. Then he opened a valve. With a huge noise, the great pump handle swung down … and up … and down. It was working!

In less than an hour, 57 feet (around 17m) of water had been pumped from the mine.

At last, eleven years after James Watt had had his great idea, his engine was a success.

Before long, James moved to Cornwall, helping to set up his engine in tin and copper mines. These mines often flooded but there was not much coal around to power the water pumps. Boulton & Watt's engine saved fuel, which was very important.

Despite the success, James did not enjoy his time in Cornwall. And neither did his new wife, Anne.

As so often happened when he was overworked, James became ill and unhappy. At such times, he could hardly think straight. He even fell out with his business partner Matthew Boulton, and wrote him bitter letters.

I'm left with all the difficult work as usual. I've a good mind to break off our agreement.

Luckily, Matthew Boulton understood that James was ill. And Mrs Watt wrote herself to make sure he didn't forget!

Meanwhile, Matthew Boulton was making other plans to use his partner's skills.

The Boulton & Watt steam engine worked with an up-and-down motion, ideal for pumping water or lifting miners to the surface.

Boulton wanted to develop an engine with a rotary motion. This would go round and round. It could power machines that made cotton fabrics and lots of other goods.

The inventor's ideas for a rotary engine filled over three metres of paper! Boulton was delighted.

Soon, there were more orders for the engine than the Boulton & Watt factory could cope with!

Boulton & Watt's fame spread far and wide. One day, James found himself explaining his engines to King George III.

As usual, James did not stop work just because his new engine was a success. He continued to try to improve it and discussed his progress with his son, James.

Success with steam engines didn't stop James Watt being interested in other subjects. At a time when all letters were written by hand, he invented a way of copying them using a special ink and a press. This method saved time and became very popular.

The inventor also noticed that there wasn't a good way of measuring how much work an engine could do. He worked out a way of comparing an engine's work with the work a horse could do. He could now describe an engine as having a certain horsepower.

James worked out that a horse could lift 33,000 pounds (15,000kg) by one foot (0.305m) in one minute.

Boulton and Watt had become rich and famous through their work on the steam engine, but that didn't mean that their troubles were at an end. Other people were always trying to steal their ideas.

The only way to protect an invention was to take out a patent. This then meant that only the inventor could make, use or sell a particular invention. But patents could be challenged and only lasted for a certain number of years.

In 1800, James Watt was sixty-four. His friend Matthew Boulton was over seventy. In the same year, their main patent ran out. It was time for the partners to retire.

This is a fine house you've built yourself, James. You can relax now with your family

But James Watt didn't stop.
He enjoyed discussing science
with his friends. He kept up with
scientific discoveries. He even
planted a garden. But most of
all, he did what he liked best …

he built himself a workshop in the attic of his new house and carried on inventing!

James lived long enough to see the world changed for ever by his steam engine and the uses of steam that followed it. The first steam locomotive travelled nine and a half miles (16kms) in 1804.

James died in 1819. Thanks to his work and the work of men like him, Britain was well on the way to being the greatest industrial country in the world.

Further facts

Power and industry

Before men like James Watt made steam engines that worked well, there were only three ways of powering any machine. You could use muscles, wind or water.

The muscles might be your own or might belong to a horse, mule or ox that walked around a treadmill. The wind or running water were used to turn the sails or wheels of mills.

Steam engines were more powerful and could be built almost anywhere. They helped to change the face of Britain for ever. Small, family businesses in the countryside gave way to large factories in towns.

Watt and watts

The *watt*, named after James Watt, is a unit of power, most often used for electrical power. A 60-watt light bulb is more powerful than a 40-watt one, for example. One horsepower – James Watt's own measurement – is equal to about 750 watts.

Some important dates in James Watt's lifetime

1736   James Watt is born in Greenock, Scotland.

1755   James goes to London to study instrument-making.

1763   A model Newcomen engine is brought to James for repair at Glasgow University.

1765   James works out a way of improving the Newcomen engine.

1774   James moves to Birmingham and goes into partnership with the factory-owner, Matthew Boulton.

1776   Boulton & Watt's steam pump makes its first appearance in public.

1783   James builds the first rotary steam engine.

1819   James Watt dies at his home near Birmingham, aged 83.